Rules of the York County Hospital, etc.

Anonymous

Rules of the York County Hospital, etc.
Anonymous
British Library, Historical Print Editions
British Library
1846
25 p. ; 8°.
10347.ee.23.(5.)

GUIDE TO FOLD-OUTS, MAPS and OVERSIZED IMAGES

In an online database, page images do not need to conform to the size restrictions found in a printed book. When converting these images back into a printed bound book, the page sizes are standardized in ways that maintain the detail of the original. For large images, such as fold-out maps, the original page image is split into two or more pages.

Guidelines used to determine the split of oversize pages:

• Some images are split vertically; large images require vertical and horizontal splits.
• For horizontal splits, the content is split left to right.
• For vertical splits, the content is split from top to bottom.
• For both vertical and horizontal splits, the image is processed from top left to bottom right.

RULES

OF THE

YORK

COUNTY HOSPITAL,

AS REVISED BY A

SPECIAL COMMITTEE,

ADOPTED BY A

GENERAL COURT OF GOVERNORS,

MAY 13TH, 1845,

AND CONFIRMED BY A

GENERAL COURT OF TRUSTEES,

FEBRUARY 10TH, 1846.

~~~~~~~~~~~~~~~~~~~~~~~~~~~

YORK:

PRINTED BY R. PICKERING, 8, SPURRIERGATE.

—

1846.

OFFICERS OF THE YORK COUNTY HOSPITAL,
1846.

TREASURER,

ROBERT SWANN, Esquire.

PHYSICIANS,

HENRY STEPHENS BELCOMBE, M. D.

THOMAS SIMPSON, M. D.

SURGEONS,

HENRY RUSSELL, Esquire.

RICHARD HEY, Esquire.

CHAPLAIN,

Rev. JOSIAH CROFTS, M. A.

STEWARD AND SECRETARY,

Mr. JOSEPH MUNBY.

APOTHECARY,

Mr. EDMUND CHARLES FRANKHAM.

MATRON,

Mrs. A. G. HARDCASTLE.

CONTENTS.

RULES

OF THE

YORK COUNTY HOSPITAL.

SECTION I.

RULES RELATING TO THE TRUSTEES OF THE HOSPITAL.

I. THE Trustees shall form a distinct and separate Court; and shall have no right to attend or vote in a Court of Governors.

II. General Courts of Trustees shall be held four times a-year; viz. on the second Tuesday in May, August, November, and February, respectively, at twelve o'clock at noon. The Quarterly Court in May shall be the Annual Court. They shall also hold a Special General Court, on notice given by the Secretary, at the instance of any three Trustees, or of the House Committee, or upon the requisition of any five Governors.

III. Not less than three Trustees shall be competent to form a General Court. The Court, whether Quarterly or Special, may appoint a Committee, consisting of at least three Trustees, to act until the next general Court, and their acts, during that time, shall be valid, provided they be consistent with the Rules.

IV.   The Court of Trustees shall have a negative on the election of the Physicians, Surgeons, Apothecary, Treasurer, Steward, and Chaplain; and on the dismissal of any of these Officers.   Their decision shall be by ballot or scroll; and if the votes be equal, the senior Trustee present shall have a casting vote.

V.   The Annual Accounts of the Hospital, when audited by the Committee of Governors, (Rule XIX.) shall be laid before the Trustees, or their Committee, previously to their being printed.

VI.   If, on stating the Accounts of the preceding year, it shall appear that the current expenses have exceeded the annual income, the Trustees shall be empowered to direct such a limitation in the number of Patients for the ensuing year, as may bring the expenses of that year within the income of the Hospital.

VII.   The sanction of the Trustees or their Committee shall be required to any expenditure in new erections, alterations, repairs, or improvements of the buildings, or on the estates of the Hospital, if such expenditure shall, in the whole, in any one quarter, exceed twenty pounds.

VIII. On the demise or resignation of a Trustee, the Quarterly Court of Trustees shall choose a new Trustee, provided that each surviving or continuing Trustee shall have received a month's notice of the vacancy. Every new Trustee shall be chosen from among the Governors, who were such at the time when the vacancy occurred.*

SECTION II.

RULES RELATING TO THE GOVERNORS OF THE HOSPITAL.

IX. EVERY Benefactor of twenty guineas, in one payment, shall be a Governor for life; † and every Annual Subscriber of two guineas and upwards, shall be a Governor during the continuance of such Subscription.

X. The Physicians, Surgeons, Steward, and Chaplain, shall be Governors ex-officio, and entitled to the same privileges as Annual Subscribers of two guineas.

---

* It is provided by the Deed of Trust, that when the Trustees named in the Deed, shall be reduced to three or fewer, a conveyance shall be made from such surviving Trustees to the use of all the subsisting Trustees duly elected, according to the Rules of the Hospital.

† Every Benefactor of Twenty Pounds, in one payment, prior to February, 1809, is also a Governor for life.

B

XI.　Every Clergyman, or Minister of a separate congregation, who shall transmit to the Treasurer a collection made by him, to the amount of two guineas, shall be a Governor for one year from the transmission of such collection, and shall be entitled during that year, to the same privileges as an Annual Subscriber of two guineas.

XII.　All Annual Subscriptions shall be payable annually in advance, and shall be considered due from the quarter day preceding the date of subscription. *　The quarter days are the 1st of May, the 1st of August, the 1st of November, and the 1st of February.

XIII.　No Governor whose annual subscription shall be three months in arrear, shall be entitled to vote at any Court of Governors.　And if, after notice of such arrear from the Secretary in writing, the subscription of any Governor shall remain one month longer unpaid, all his privileges as a Governor shall be suspended, till his arrear be paid.

COURT OF GOVERNORS.

XIV.　THE Governors shall form a distinct and separate Court.　Not less than five Governors shall constitute a Court.

_____

* The Annual Subscriptions of all persons who subscribed before the 10th of November, 1818, are due on the 1st of May, in each year.

xv. General Quarterly Courts of Governors shall be held on the second Tuesday in May, August, November, and February, respectively, at twelve o'clock at noon. The Quarterly Court in May shall be the Annual Court. Special General Courts shall also be held, on notice given by the Secretary, at the instance of any three Trustees, or of the House Committee, or upon the requisition of any five Governors.

xvi. Notice of every Court of Governors shall be given by the Secretary, once in each of the York Newspapers.

xvii. The Court shall proceed to business as soon after twelve o'clock as five Governors shall have assembled. But if five Governors be not present at half-past twelve, no Court shall be held on that day; and the Governors present, or the Steward, shall fix a day for holding a Special Court, until which time, the Visitors of the preceding quarter, and if it be the Annual Court, the former House Committee, shall continue to act.

xviii. Every Court shall choose its Chairman by ballot or scroll; the Annual Court shall appoint the House Committee, and each Quarterly Court the Visitors, before any other business be entered upon.

xix. At each Quarterly Court, in February, a

Committee of three Governors shall be appointed to audit the Accounts, to draw up the Report, and to superintend the printing of the same. The Accounts, when audited, shall be signed by the Chairman of the Audit Committee, and laid before the Trustees or their Committee. The Report, with the Accounts annexed, shall be printed, and ready for distribution at or before each Annual Court.

xx. No new Rule shall be adopted, nor any existing Rule altered or repealed, except at the Annual Court, nor unless a written notice shall have been given at the preceding Quarterly Court; and the enactment, alteration, or repeal of any Rule shall not be valid, until submitted to the Court of Trustees, and sanctioned by their signature. Immediately after each Annual Court, the House Committee shall cause to be printed the alterations which have been made in the Rules, in such form that they may be attached to the printed copies.

xxi. The Court shall have the cognizance and direction of all matters relating to the receipt or disbursement of money for the Hospital, except in the case specified in Rule vii.

xxii. The Court shall have the power of electing the Officers in the mode hereafter prescribed, subject to the confirmation of the Trustees.

XXIII. The Court may, from time to time, make such regulations as they think necessary, relative to the admission and discharge of patients, and the management of the Institution, provided they be consistent with the Rules.

XXIV. Every Resolution of the Court of Governors, requiring the sanction of the Trustees, shall be signed by five Governors in the name of the whole, and be carried by them to the Court of Trustees.

HOUSE COMMITTEE.

XXV. THE House Committee shall consist of seven Governors, and shall be elected by ballot or scroll, at the Annual Court.

XXVI. Any Court of Governors may make such changes in their Committee, as they shall find necessary; and each Quarterly Court shall fill up such vacancies as may occur by removal or resignation, or by non-attendance during a quarter, which shall be considered equivalent to resignation. If any of the Governors elected at any time, shall decline to act, the other Members of the Committee may fill up the vacancies till the next Quarterly Court.

XXVII. No Officer of the Institution shall be on this Committee; and no Member of this Committee shall be employed in the erection, repair, or alteration of buildings, or in supplying furniture, medicines, stores, or provisions to the Hospital.

xxviii.   Each Governor elected a Member of this Committee, shall have notice thereof given him by the Secretary.

xxix.   The Committee shall choose a Chairman at their first Meeting, and may be called together at any time by the Secretary at his own discretion, or when directed by the Chairman.   There shall be stated Meetings of the Committee on the second Tuesday of every month.   Not less than three members shall constitute a Quorum.

xxx.   The Committee shall every month examine such bills as are brought in, and sanction them, if approved, by their signature; they shall also, every quarter, give an order on the Treasurer for the sum wanted to pay the bills which are approved; and at their first meeting in the following quarter, shall have the Steward's accounts of the preceding quarter, with the bills and receipts, laid before them.

xxxi.   The Committee shall possess, during the intervals of the Courts, all the powers of the Court of Governors, except as to the election or dismissal of Officers, and the enactment or alteration of Rules.

VISITORS AND BOARD.

XXXII.   EACH Quarterly Court of Governors shall appoint six Gentlemen, being Governors resident in York or the immediate neighbourhood, to be Visitors of the Hospital for the ensuing quarter, two for each month.

XXXIII.   Each Quarterly Court of Governors shall appoint six Ladies, resident in York or the immediate neighbourhood, to be Visitors of the Female Wards for the ensuing quarter, two for each month.

XXXIV.   It shall be the duty of the Visitors, to visit the Wards, and to inspect the state of the House, and the conduct of the patients and servants.

XXXV.   A Letter shall be addressed by the Chairman of the Court to each Governor appointed a Visitor, stating his or her appointment, and if any of them decline to officiate, the House Committee shall appoint others in their place.

XXXVI.   The House Committee, the Visitors for the quarter, and such other Governors as choose to attend, shall constitute a Board, whose business shall be to regulate all matters relating to the admission and discharge of patients.   The Board shall meet on Thursdays, precisely at twelve o'clock, and the

Medical Officers shall be prepared to report at that hour on all cases of application for admission, and on all cases for discharge.

XXXVII. Books shall be kept for the entry of observations by the Visitors, and for recording the proceedings of the Board, which shall be submitted to the Governors at each Quarterly Court.

SECTION III.

RULES RELATING TO THE PATIENTS.

RIGHT OF RECOMMENDING PATIENTS.

XXXVIII. EVERY Benefactor of thirty guineas, or Annual Subscriber of three guineas, shall be allowed to have one in-patient and one out-patient on the books at a time. Every Benefactor of twenty guineas * or Annual Subscriber of two guineas, shall be allowed one in-patient or one out-patient on the books at a time. And every Benefactor of ten guineas, or Annual Subscriber of one guinea, shall be allowed to have one out-patient only.

XXXIX. The Physicians and Surgeons, the Chaplain and Steward, ex-officio, and every Clergyman and Minister in virtue of a collection made by him,

---

* Every Benefactor of Twenty Pounds, in one payment, prior to February, 1809, has the same privilege of recommendation as a Benefactor of Twenty Guineas.

shall respectively have the same privilege of recommendation with an Annual Subscriber of two guineas. (Rules x, xi.)

xl. The acting Overseer of any parish which pays an annual subscription of two guineas, shall have the same privilege with a Subscriber of the like sum, so far as relates to the recommendation of patients.

xli. No Subscriber shall exercise the privilege of recommending patients, unless his subscription and all arrears, if there be any, shall be paid, according to Rules xii. and xiii. The Steward shall give notice of such suspension of privilege to the Apothecary. (Rule lxxi.)

xlii. Every Benefactor or Annual Subscriber desirous of recommending as an in-patient, a person residing at a distance, is requested to send to the Apothecary a written statement of the patient's case, to which the Apothecary shall be directed to return an answer, stating whether and at what time the patient can be admitted.

ADMISSION OF PATIENTS.

xliii. Patients having recommendations, shall attend at the Hospital on a Thursday, at half-past ten in the forenoon.

XLIV.   The Physician and Surgeon of the week shall examine the patients, and report to the Board what cases are proper to be admitted as in-patients, or made out-patients.   But if no members of the Board be present, the Physician and Surgeon of the week shall have the power to admit patients.

XLV.   When there is a scarcity of beds in the Hospital, the most urgent cases shall be first admitted, and the rest according to priority of application.

XLVI.   No patient shall be admitted without a proper recommendation, except cases of accident, which may be admitted at all times, without recommendation.

XLVII.   Children under seven years of age shall not be admitted in-patients, except those whose cases require some important surgical operation.

XLVIII.   No person of known profligate character, or having the venereal disease, or any infectious or contagious disorder, shall be admitted an in-patient.

XLIX.   If a patient bringing a recommendation, cannot be admitted into the Hospital, the Apothecary shall by letter state the reason thereof to the Benefactor or Subscriber who gave the recommendation.

L. The in-patients shall submit themselves to the direction of their respective Physician or Surgeon, the Apothecary, and the Matron; and shall conduct themselves orderly, and observe the Rules, as long as they remain in the Hospital. The out-patients are to attend regularly at the times appointed by the Apothecary.

LI. If any infectious fever occur in the Hospital, the patient shall be instantly removed to the Fever-Ward. And if any other infectious or contagious disorder occur, the medical officers shall, at their discretion, either remove the patient to the Fever-Ward, or make him an out-patient.

DISCHARGE OF PATIENTS.

LII. No patient shall remain in the Hospital longer than medical attendance can be of service to him.

LIII. Every in-patient shall be discharged at the end of one calendar month after his admission, unless the Physician or Surgeon under whose care such patient may be placed, shall certify to the Committee, in writing, a satisfactory reason why he should not be removed; and if the patient should remain one month longer, a fresh certificate shall be required.

LIV. If any patient shall have been admitted in contravention of any Rule of the Hospital, or shall have behaved disorderly, the Board or the Committee shall order the dismissal of such patient: but he shall not be removed, if the proper medical officer certify, that his removal will be attended with serious danger. The Physician or Surgeon under whose care the patient is placed, or in his absence, the Apothecary, if necessary, shall have the same power of dismissal.

LV. On the discharge of any patient, the Apothecary shall by letter sent through the post, state to the Benefactor or Subscriber, who gave the recommendation, the reason of the patient's discharge.

SECTION IV.

RULES RELATING TO THE OFFICERS OF THE HOSPITAL.

LVI. THE Officers of this Institution shall be two Physicians; two Surgeons; an Apothecary, who shall also be Librarian; a Treasurer; a Steward, who shall also act as Secretary; and a Chaplain.

ELECTION AND REMOVAL OF OFFICERS.

LVII. ON the occurrence of a vacancy by the death, resignation, or removal of any Officer, the Secretary (or if his office be vacant, the Apothecary) shall, immediately on being apprized thereof, convene a Meeting of the House Committee of Governors, to declare the vacancy. The Committee shall give at least a month's notice, once in each of the York Newspapers, of the election, which shall take place at a Special Court of Trustees and Governors.

LVIII. Every Candidate shall deliver his testimonials to the House Committee, at least one week before the day of election: and the Committee shall desire the attendance of the Physicians and Surgeons, to examine the testimonials of every Candidate for a medical office.

LIX. No Court of Governors for the election or removal of any Officer, shall be held sooner than one o'clock.

LX. In the election or removal of any Officer, no Governor shall be admitted to vote, who shall not have become a Governor six months before such vote be tendered, or whose subscription is three months in arrear. (See Rules XII, XIII.)

LXI. The election or removal of any Officer shall be decided by ballot or scroll; and if the votes be equal, the Chairman shall have the casting vote.

LXII. If the Court of Trustees shall refuse to confirm the election of any Officer by the Court of Governors, the Physicians, Surgeons, Treasurer, Secretary, and Chaplain, or such of them as shall remain in office, shall, within one week, hold a meeting, at which they shall appoint any fit person (except the rejected Candidate) to do the duties of the vacant office, until it be regularly supplied.

PHYSICIANS AND SURGEONS.

LXIII. THE Physicians and Surgeons shall attend on Mondays and Thursdays, at eleven o'clock, A. M.; and one Physician and one Surgeon shall take the duty, by weekly rotation, of examining the patients for admission.

LXIV. The Physician and the Surgeon of the week, shall each have the exclusive care of the patients admitted, according as the cases are medical or surgical. But in cases of a mixed nature, the Physician and Surgeon shall have the joint care; and in difficult or protracted cases, a consultation of all the Physicians and Surgeons shall be held, that the best method of treatment may be adopted.

LXV. Before any important surgical operation is performed, notice shall be sent by the Apothecary, to all the Physicians and Surgeons, and a consultation held; unless the case be so urgent, as not to admit of such delay.

LXVI. The Physicians and Surgeons shall be allowed to introduce pupils to attend the medical and surgical practice of the Hospital: but they shall first give in the name of each to the Quarterly Court or the House Committee, and obtain their permission: and the Court or Committee may prohibit the further attendance of any pupil, who shall misconduct himself.

LXVII. If a Physician or Surgeon be necessarily absent from his duty at the Hospital for a period not exceeding three months, he shall make an arrangement with his Colleague to officiate for him; but if his absence shall exceed three months, or his Colleague decline to officiate, then the Court of Governors, with the consent of the Trustees, shall appoint a temporary substitute; and at the end of a year, if he shall not have resumed his duty, his office shall be declared vacant.

APOTHECARY.

LXVIII. THE Apothecary (who shall also act as Librarian) shall have served a regular apprenticeship to his profession, and shall satisfy the Physicians and Surgeons as to his competency. His age at election shall be between thirty and forty-five years.

LXIX. He shall reside in the Hospital, and receive a Salary, and shall not engage in private practice. He shall be master of the household, and, as such, shall be responsible to the House Committee for the order and good government of the household. He shall keep the keys of the house and see that the doors be locked according to the rules. He shall not be absent for a night, without the permission of the Physicians and Surgeons; and when absent at any time, shall leave directions with the Matron where he may be found.

LXX. He shall keep a correct list of all Subscribers and Benefactors who have the right of recommending patients.

LXXI. He shall keep a register, stating the Name, Age, Parish, Recommendation, and Date of admission of every in and out-patient; and the Physician and Surgeon under whose care they are respectively admitted.

LXXII. He shall place over the bed of each in-patient, a Ticket stating the above particulars, and the Diet prescribed.

LXXIII. If a patient bringing a Recommendation, cannot be admitted into the Hospital, the Apothecary shall by letter state the reason thereof to the

Benefactor or Subscriber who gave the Recommendation.

LXXIV. On the discharge of every in or out-patient, he shall make an entry thereof in the register, and state the same by letter, to the Benefactor or Subscriber who recommended the patient, with the reason of the patient's discharge.

LXXV. He shall visit the Wards every morning and evening, when he shall call over the names of the patients, and enter in a book, to be produced to the Visitors or House Committee, such as are absent, or have transgressed any Rule.

LXXVI. He shall not admit or give advice or Medicines to any patients who are not regularly recommended, except in cases of accident, as hereafter provided.

LXXVII. He shall be in readiness to attend the Physicians and Surgeons at their visits; and, as soon as possible after each visit, shall examine the prescription-book, and make up and dispense the Medicines prescribed.

LXXVIII. He shall daily dispense the Medicines prescribed for the in-patients, and attend to every direction of the Physicians and Surgeons relating to the medical treatment and regimen of the patients:

but if any unforeseen change in the state of a patient shall occur in the absence of the Physicians and Surgeons, he may administer such remedies as the urgency of the case may require.

LXXIX.   He shall have the charge of the surgical instruments and the shop utensils, and shall keep an inventory of them.   He shall enter the names and quantities of all medicines wanted, in a book, which shall be signed by two of the medical officers, before such medicines are ordered ; and shall keep a checkbook of all articles brought into the house on the shop account; which inventory and books shall be open to the inspection of the House Committee and Medical Officers.

LXXX.   The Apothecary shall be allowed to take a pupil, provided the individual be approved by the Medical Officers, and provided the consent of the Quarterly Court or House Committee be obtained. The Court or Committee may prohibit the further attendance at the Hospital of any pupil who shall misconduct himself.   No pupil shall lodge or be boarded in the Hospital.

TREASURER.

LXXXI.   THE Treasurer shall keep a separate Account at one of the York Banks, to be called the Account of the Treasurer of the York County Hospital; and all sums received by the Treasurer or

Steward, on behalf of the Institution, shall be paid into the Bank to the credit of such account.

LXXXII. The Treasurer shall receive all legacies and donations, and give discharges for them : he shall also receive the dividends on the money in the funds and shall issue checks for money to the Steward, when the House Committee shall direct : and in the Treasurer's absence from York, the Chairman of the House Committee may give such checks.

LXXXIII. Any Donation or Legacy, if given or bequeathed expressly for the purpose of being funded, shall be accepted, and funded accordingly; but if given or bequeathed, subject to any other condition, qualification, or restriction, it shall not be accepted, unless with the approbation of a Quarterly or Special General Court.

LXXXIV. All Legacies exceeding twenty guineas, and all Donations given upon the express condition of being funded, shall be invested in the names of Trustees, in a distinct and separate account from the other funds of the Institution. The principal of the funds thus specially invested, shall not be applied to make good any deficiency in the annual income, but shall ever remain invested at interest, with power to change the securities for the same, at the discretion of the General Courts. A report of all such legacies and donations shall be laid before every Quarterly

Court by the Steward, in order that this Rule may be carried into effect.

LXXXV. The Treasurer shall keep for the use of the Trustees, a key of the chest wherein the Deeds, Rules, and Minutes of the Institution are deposited.

STEWARD AND SECRETARY.

LXXXVI. THE Steward shall, within a month after his election, give to the Treasurer a security to such amount as shall be satisfactory to the House Committee.

LXXXVII. He shall take charge of the collection of Subscriptions, Rents, and other Monies, as they become due, and shall pay all Monies that come into his hands for the Hospital, to the Treasurer's account at least once a month.

LXXXVIII. He shall pay such Bills as are signed by the House Committee, as soon as possible after he shall have received money from the Treasurer for that purpose, and shall keep a regular account of his receipts and expenditure, and produce it when called upon by a Court of Governors, the House Committee, or the Treasurer.

LXXXIX. He shall lay before every Quarterly Court a report of all Legacies and Donations received, which come within Rule LXXXIV, in order that the said Rule may be carried into effect.

xc. He shall every year make out a statement, under proper heads, of all the Receipts and Disbursements on account of the Hospital, and lay the same before the Audit Committee. (See Rule XIX.)

xci. He shall give, in writing, notice to every Governor, whose annual subscription shall remain unpaid three months after the time when it shall have become due. And if the subscription remain in arrear one month after such notice, the Steward shall inform the Apothecary of such arrear. (See Rules XII, XIII, XLI.)

xcii. He shall summon the General Courts, and the Committees of Trustees and Governors, and keep minutes of their proceedings.

xciii. On the demise or resignation of a Trustee, the Steward shall give notice to each continuing Trustee, for filling up the vacancy at the first Quarterly Court which shall be held after the end of one month from the notice of such vacancy.

xciv. He shall keep, for the use of the Governors, a key of the chest wherein the Deeds, Rules, and Minutes of the Hospital are deposited.

CHAPLAIN.

xcv. The Chaplain shall read Prayers in the Hall, on Sunday and on some other day in every week; and shall require the attendance of such

patients as are able to quit the wards. He shall
visit the sick in the wards at least once in every
week; and shall take care that proper religious books
be provided for the use of the patients.

SECTION V.

RULES RELATING TO THE MATRON;

AND TO THE NURSES AND SERVANTS.

xcvi. The House Committee shall appoint or remove the Matron, Nurses, and Servants, at their
discretion.

xcvii. The Matron shall keep an inventory of the
household goods, linen, and furniture, and give an
account thereof when required.

xcviii. She shall examine, weigh, and measure
all provisions and stores brought into the house,
except such as belong to the Apothecary's depart-
ment; and shall keep a check-book of all such
provisions and stores, to be laid before the House
Committee at their meetings.

xcix. She shall deliver out provisions in such
quantities as shall be directed, and shall strictly
adhere to the rule of diet prescribed for each patient.
She shall keep a journal of the diet of the patients,
and the consumption of provisions, according to a

form to be fixed by the House Committee, and lay it before them at their meetings.

c.   She shall visit each ward every day, and shall take care that the patients' apparel, bed-linen, and bedding, be kept clean.

ci.   She shall not be absent at the same time as the Apothecary.

cii.   She shall see that the nurses, servants, and patients, observe the Rules of the House, and do their duty.—The nurses and servants shall obey the Apothecary and Matron, as master and mistress of the House.

ciii.   The nurses shall punctually observe the orders of the Physicians and Surgeons, and shall report to them, or to the Apothecary or Matron, every instance of misconduct in the patients.

civ.   The friends of the patients shall be allowed to visit them, at such times, and under such restrictions, as the House Committee shall appoint.

cv.   No money, fee, or reward, shall be taken from patients or their friends, on pain of dismissal.

cvi.   The doors of the House shall be locked at nine in winter and ten in summer.

R. Pickering, Printer, 8, Spurriergate, York.

Lightning Source UK Ltd.
Milton Keynes UK
UKHW032003030822
406816UK00010B/97